W9-BCU-306

Riches of the Earth

Silver

Irene Franck and David Brownstone

GROLIER

An imprint of Scholastic Library Publishing
Danbury, Connecticut

Credits and Acknowledgments

abbreviations: t (top), b (bottom), l (left), r (right), c (center)

Image credits: Art Resource: 3 (Victoria and Albert Museum), 4 (Newark Museum, Gift of the Vivienne and Stanley H. Katz Fund); 7, 9, 15, and 24b (Erich Lessing); 10 (Pierpont Morgan Library), 21l (Newark Museum), 24t (Scala), 25; Bancroft Library (University of California, Berkeley): 17; CORBIS: 21r (Ralph White), 26 (Bettman); Getty Images: 22 (PhotoDisc/David Buffington), 27 (Stone/Gavin Wilson), 28 (Stone/Eva Mueller); National Aeronautics and Space Administration (NASA): 1t and running heads, 29; Photo Researchers, Inc.: 8l (Alan Carruthers), 8r (Tom McHugh), 11 and 18 (Porterfield/Pickering), 12 and 20 (Ted Clutter); Southwest Indian Foundation (Ted Ellefson): 1b, 5l, 5r; Woodfin Camp & Associates: 6 (Michal Bryant), 13l and 13r (Kal Muller), 14 (George Whiteley), 19 (Mireille Vautier), 23 (Frank Fournier). Original image drawn for this book by K & P Publishing Services: 16.

Our thanks to Joe Hollander, Phil Friedman, and Laurie McCurley at Scholastic Library Publishing; to photo researchers Susan Hormuth, Robin Sand, and Robert Melcak; to copy editor Michael Burke; and to the librarians throughout the northeastern library network, in particular to the staff of the Chappaqua Library—director Mark Hasskarl; the expert reference staff, including Martha Alcott, Michele J. Capozzella, Maryanne Eaton, Catherine Paulsen, Jane Peyraud, Paula Peyraud, and Carolyn Reznick; and the circulation staff, headed by Barbara Le Sauvage—for fulfilling our wide-ranging research needs.

Published 2003 by Grolier
Division of Scholastic Library Publishing
Old Sherman Turnpike
Danbury, Connecticut 06816

For information address the publisher:
Scholastic Library Publishing, Grolier Division
Old Sherman Turnpike, Danbury, Connecticut 06816

© 2003 Irene M. Franck and David M. Brownstone

All rights reserved. Except for use in a review, no part of this book may be reproduced, stored in a retrieval system, or transmitted in any form, or by any means, electronic or mechanical, including photocopying, recording, or otherwise, without prior permission of Scholastic Library Publishing.

Library of Congress Cataloging-in-Publication Data

Franck, Irene M.
    Silver / Irene Franck and David Brownstone.
      p. cm. -- (Riches of the earth ; v. 12)
    Summary: Provides information about silver and its importance in everyday life.
    Includes bibliographical references and index.
    ISBN 0-7172-5730-4 (set : alk. paper) -- ISBN 0-7172-5724-X (vol. 12 : alk paper)
      1. Silver--Juvenile literature [1. Silver.] I. Brownstone, David M. II. Title.

TN761.6.F734 2003
669'.23--dc21

2003044090

Printed in the United States of America

Designed by K & P Publishing Services

Contents

Silver and gold have sometimes been used together in the same object. This covered punch bowl from the late 1800s is primarily of silver, but it is decorated with leaves that are gilded (covered with gold).

Silver and Gold

Silver has often taken a backseat to gold. Though usually less highly prized than gold, silver has for thousands of years been one of the most valuable metals. In many countries someone from a rich family is said to have been "born with a silver spoon in his mouth." That's because a silver spoon or cup was a traditional gift for a new baby.

Silver has been widely used over the centuries as money, in jewelry, and in other items of value, such as candlesticks and plates in rich households. Even today, our knives, forks, and spoons are still often called "silverware," though most are no longer made of silver. In the same way coins are often called "silver," though today most contain no silver at all (see p. 24).

Gold has long been linked with the sun, especially the brilliant dawn. By contrast, grayish-white silver has traditionally been linked with the moon and its ghostly light. Indeed, alchemists—early scientists who tried to make precious metals out of other substances—used a special symbol to represent silver: the shape of a new moon.

You probably know that silver is

One of the reasons that silver is so prized for jewelry is that it reflects back so much light. The Native-American silversmith who made this silver necklace called it *liquid silver*, because it reflects light as the water does on a sunny day.

For many centuries a traditional gift for a new baby was a silver spoon or cup, like this modern baby's cup made by Native-American silversmiths.

used in jewelry and in fillings in your teeth. But you may not know that silver also has many other uses. One of the most important modern industrial uses has been in photographic film (see p. 26). This is because some silver-containing materials are extremely sensitive to light. Silver's light sensitivity is also used in special sunglasses that darken in bright light and lighten in dimmer light. Much silver is also used in the electronics industry.

Most of all, silver is just plain beautiful. Polished silver seems to shine, because it reflects (throws back) so much of the light around it. That makes it perfect for use in jewelry, whether as simple, stylish silver objects or as settings for precious stones, such as diamonds, and semiprecious stones, such as turquoise.

What Is Silver?

The beauty of highly reflective, shining silver always catches the eye. This gleaming silver writing set, including an old-fashioned quill pen and ink holder, is on display in Philadelphia's Independence Hall, where the Declaration of Independence and the U.S. Constitution (shown in the background) were written.

The gleaming grayish-white color of silver is well known. Many things are described as being of a silver color, when they are not made of silver at all. The real silver is a very special material.

Every living and nonliving thing on the Earth is made up of some basic materials called elements (we know of 112 so far, though more are being discovered). Silver is one of those *elements*—and rather a rare one. It is found in many places on Earth but only in very small amounts overall. How rare is it? If you divided the Earth's crust (the

Silversmiths in Europe and Asia were highly skilled from very early times. This rhyton (a special drinking vessel) in the shape of a ram's bust was found in Turkey and dates from between 900 and 500 B.C.

outer part that we live on) into 100 million pieces, only five of them would be made of silver!

Silver as a Metal

Silver is one of a group of elements called *metals*. Many metals allow heat and electricity to flow through them very readily. Scientists call these *good conductors*. Silver is the best conductor of them all. However, it is used primarily in high-quality electrical and electronic equipment. It is too rare and expensive for everyday use in household wiring.

Like gold and platinum, silver is called one of the *precious metals*, because they are all highly prized

for use in jewelry and coins. Indeed, silver was for centuries the metal most widely used for coins (see p. 24). That is because silver does not readily *corrode* (dissolve or wear away) in normal use and it generally resists *tarnishing* (dulling or discoloring).

Like most other metals, silver is solid at room temperature. Silver is little affected by extreme temperature changes, and it does not melt until the temperature tops 962 degrees Celsius (about 1764 degrees Fahrenheit). This means that silver can be used in a very wide range of situations.

Once melted, however, silver can be poured into molds of desired

When silver is heated to above 962 degrees Celsius (about 1764 degrees Fahrenheit), it melts. Then it can be poured into molds (left), sometimes forming bars called ingots (below).

shapes. It can also be joined with other elements to form mixed materials called *compounds*.

Many metals join together readily to form compounds (chemists call this *reacting*). Indeed, silver forms some very important compounds widely used in industry (see p. 26). However, in everyday use, silver does not react with most substances. Silver does not corrode when exposed to oxygen and water (unlike iron, which combines with oxygen in the air to form rust). Because of this, silver (again like gold and platinum) is labeled one of the *noble metals*, so called because they "stand apart" as nobles and other lords are thought to do.

Silver does, however, easily react with the element sulfur. The air usually contains small amounts of *sul-*

fur, so silver objects will come to be covered with a yellowish-black film called *tarnish*. That's why objects made of silver need to be cleaned periodically, to remove the tarnish and restore the shine.

Tarnishing usually happens slowly. However, modern polluted air (which contains more sulfur) causes more rapid tarnishing. Tarnishing also occurs more quickly if silver is left in contact with a sulfur-containing substance, as when a silver fork is left sitting in egg or mustard.

Soft Silver

Silver is also prized because it is so soft and easy to work. It is very *malleable*—that is, it can easily be formed into desired shapes. It is also very *ductile*—that is, it can easily be drawn into thin wires or hammered into thin sheets, without crushing or shattering. Silver can be used to form fine threads, sometimes coated with gold. Such threads have been used over the centuries in rich tapestries and expensive robes and gowns.

However, silver all by itself is too soft for many purposes. Partly because of that, few objects are made of pure silver. Instead, silver is usually mixed with other materials, especially metals such as copper, to give it more strength. Such metal mixtures are called *alloys*.

The problem is that, for most of history, users could not tell how much silver an object really con-

This silver cup from the Roman city of Pompeii was buried by lava from Italy's Mt. Vesuvius volcano in 79 A.D. However, after modern archaeologists rediscovered and cleaned it, the cup shone as if it were new.

tained. Therefore, they did not know its true value. That changed in the 1860s with the widespread adoption of the *sterling* standard of purity for silver compounds.

Sterling Silver

For measuring purposes silver is divided into 1,000 parts. The highest standard form of silver alloy contains 925 parts pure silver and 75 parts of other substances (often copper). Putting it another way, the highest-grade silver alloy contains 92.5 percent silver. This grade is called *sterling silver*.

Most silver used in jewelry today is not sterling, for it often has only about 800 parts (80 percent) silver. The silver alloy used in filling teeth has only about 600 to 700 parts (60 to 70 percent) silver, combined with

Silver or Ag

Scientists use a special abbreviation for silver: *Ag*. That is because the Romans (who spoke Latin) knew silver as *argentum*. They brought so much silver to Rome (in what is now Italy) from Spain that the coastal road between the two regions was called *Via Argenta* (Road of Silver).

Even after the Roman Empire fell, Latin remained the language of learning in Europe for centuries. That's why scientists continued to use the word *argentum* and one of the main silver-bearing ores is called *argentite* (see p. 12).

When Europeans later arrived in the Americas, they sent back home enormous amounts of silver. So much South American silver poured through the port of Buenos Aires that the surrounding country was named for it: *Argentina*. That country's main river, the Rio de la Plata (River Plate), also means "River of Silver," because *plate* is another word for household goods made of silver.

These Roman silver cups date from the first century. The silver probably came from Spain, in the days when the road between there and Rome was called the *Via Argenta* (Road of Silver).

In addition to its beauty, silver is prized because it sets off precious and semiprecious stones such as the blueish-green turquoise in many of these bracelets made by Navajo silversmiths.

mercury to form a mixture called an *amalgam*.

Since the 1860s objects made of sterling silver generally have had the word *sterling* on them, as a mark of quality. The word *sterling* comes from early England. In the late 700s English kings issued pennies made of 925 parts silver and 75 parts copper. The word *sterling* may have come from the Old English word *steorling*, meaning "coin with a star," since some early English coins featured stars. One pound of silver was used to make 240 pennies. That's why the British still call their main money unit the *pound sterling*.

This miner is working a drill in a modern silver mine. The dark bluish-gray ore is the kind of "damned blue stuff" that early gold miners rejected, not knowing that it was actually highly valuable silver ore.

Where Is Silver Found?

In the 1850s many gold-seekers passed through Nevada's Carson River valley on their way to California. Some stayed for a time, looking for gold. However, the small traces of gold were overwhelmed by what they called "black sand" or even "that damned blue stuff."

These gold-seekers did not realize that the bluish-gray rock they tossed aside was really the main kind of silver-bearing rock, called *argentite*. Just a few years later the Carson River valley would be home to one of the world's greatest silver mines, the Comstock Lode.

Sources of Silver

Silver is one of the few elements that is sometimes found in nearly pure form, called *native silver*. It is also sometimes found combined with gold in a naturally occurring compound called *electrum*, which is at least 20 percent silver. Most of the silver that humans found and used

In some places miners still pan for silver, as they might for gold. Taking gravel from a streambed, they swirl it around in a pan. The water flies over the side, but the heavier grains or nuggets of silver (or gold) remain behind. Panning in Mexico, this miner found the small silver nuggets shown in his hand (top left).

in early times was in one of these two forms.

Modern miners have made occasional finds of native silver, most notably in Norway and Canada. However, such near-surface sources of native silver or electrum have now been largely used up.

Silver is more often found mixed with other substances in rock formations called *ores*. Silver is usually a very minor portion of the ore, however, often less than 1 percent. Even so, it is worth mining because silver is so valuable.

Silver is especially attracted to

sulfur (see p. 8). As a result, it is often found mixed with compounds containing sulfur. In fact, argentite, the main silver ore, is made up of silver and sulfur.

Silver is often found in ores with gold and other metals, such as copper, lead, and zinc. The rocks containing them were formed by the same processes very early in the Earth's history. The core (center) of the Earth was so hot that it was liquid (as it still is). Over many millions of years, some of the liquid reached the surface and cooled to form rocks containing silver and other substances.

Over still more millions of years, some such rocks near the surface were worn down and broken apart by water, wind, rain, and other natural forces, a process called *erosion*. These forces exposed some silver ores at the surface.

Much silver-bearing rock still remained below the surface, however. Because of that, miners today sometimes have to dig deep underground to bring out silver-bearing ores.

Silver is naturally a crystal—that is, it would tend to form a shape with flat, regular sides. However, silver in crystal form is rare, because the rock carrying it was formed under such great pressure. More often silver is found in branching formations called *dendrites*, which look like thin tree twigs.

Early Silver Sources

The region of Anatolia (now Turkey) was a good early source of silver. Some of the earliest known uses of silver occurred in that region.

The Greek city of Athens had silver mines nearby. These were so rich that the playwright Aeschylus called them "fountains running silver."

The key source of silver for the Romans was the region now known as Spain. That silver helped fund the growth of the Roman Empire. When the Spanish silver began to run out late in the life of the Roman Empire, a financial crisis resulted. The government called in many coins and melted them down to make new ones containing less silver.

Things only got worse in Europe in the centuries after the fall of the Roman Empire. Little new silver

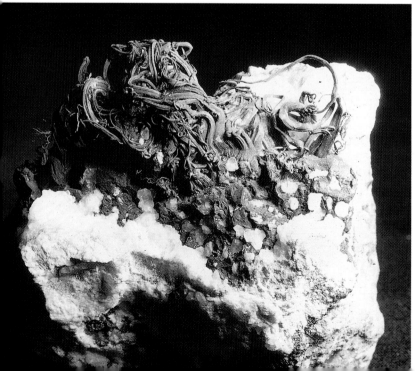

This is an example of native silver in tendril form, in the upper left part of a chunk of argentite, the main silver-bearing ore. Silver is found in many parts of the world. This sample comes from Sardinia, a large island in the Mediterranean Sea.

These are the modern remains of an ancient Greek silver mine, dating back to the sixth century B.C., more than 2,500 years ago. Crushed ore and water were sent washing down this channel. The heavier silver would sink and be held in the cups, while the water and lighter materials, such as soil, would flow on out of the channel.

was mined in Europe for some centuries, though some new sources were found in Germany.

After the Roman Empire fell, Europeans could not rely on the value of coins, which contained less and less silver. However, when European traders reached out into Asia, they found that the peoples of Asia had many fine objects of silver. Europeans were surprised to find these "not inferior to our own."

Silver in the Americas

The Europeans found major new sources of silver when they began to conquer the Americas. The Spanish took control of many rich silver sources, especially in Mexico, Peru, and Bolivia.

The Spanish shipped enormous amounts of silver (and gold) back to Europe. Eager for a share of these riches, other countries—and pirates—often attacked Spanish ships en route to Europe.

Main regions producing and using silver, past and present

Spanish ships sailed together in huge convoys. Even so, they were not safe. In the most daring and successful raid, a Dutch fleet under Piet Heyn captured the whole Spanish silver fleet in 1628, taking millions of dollars' worth of silver.

Silver Rushes

The search for silver-bearing ores was constant from very early times. Silver strikes could inspire "rushes," where people from far distant places literally rushed in, seeking to get rich.

Some of the most notable modern finds of silver have been made in countries settled by European colonists. One such strike was made in 1750 in Australia's Broken Hill region, now in New South Wales.

Many other silver strikes were made in North America. The most notable was the Comstock Lode, recognized in 1859 as a major source of silver. Miners from around the world rushed to the site at Virginia City, Nevada. As in most rushes, however, only a few became really rich.

Many of these silver sources have long since been mined out. Today mines devoted to silver alone are rare. Instead, about three-quarters

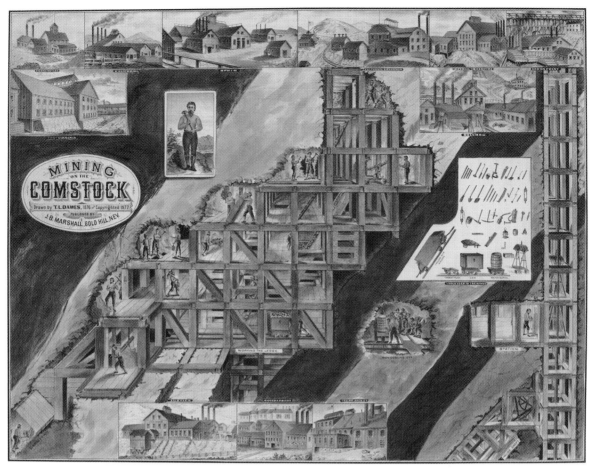

Much of the free silver available on the surface was used up in earlier times. In modern times miners have had to dig deep underground to find new silver deposits. This is a cutaway view of the famous Comstock mine in 1877.

of the silver mined each year now comes as a by-product of mining for other metals, especially copper, lead, and zinc. In modern silver mining the ore is first crushed by heavy machines. Then various methods, often involving chemical baths, are used to separate the silver and other metals from the ore.

The largest producer of silver today is Canada. Mexico, the United States, Peru, Russia, and Australia are also among the top producers.

Notable silver reserves have also been found elsewhere, as in Kazakhstan in Central Asia.

The demand for silver far outstrips the supply of the precious metal, however. That is why a large portion of each year's silver supply now comes from recycling used products containing silver, especially photographic film, solutions from photographic processing (see p. 26), old jewelry, and electrical equipment.

This modern Danish silversmith is using a small hammer to shape a silver platter cover. A finished example of his work is on the shelf in the background.

Working with Silver

We do not know when people first started using silver. We know that people in Anatolia (now Turkey) were making jewelry and other ornaments of silver by at least 4000 B.C., more than 6,000 years ago.

Along with gold and copper, silver was one of the first metals used by humans. That is because small amounts of nearly pure silver are sometimes found in nature. How-ever, silver is more often found in ores containing several kinds of valuable metals (see p. 12). Humans had to learn to extract (separate out) the silver, using a process called *smelting*.

The basic method of smelting is simple. Crushed into manageable pieces, the ore is heated in some kind of furnace until parts of it melt. Some parts turn into gases. The desired metals melt at different temperatures, so they are removed at different times during the smelting process.

Chemical Processing

Later metalworkers learned to extract silver by applying various chemicals to the rock. Over centuries they have developed special knowledge about which chemicals to apply and for how long.

In the Americas the Spanish used the *patio process*, pioneered by Native Americans. This involved having mules going round and round a circular paved floor (*patio*), crushing silver ore underfoot. When the ore was almost mudlike, they added salt, copper ore, and mercury. The silver dissolved in the mercury. Finally the mixture would be heated, driving off the mercury and leaving the silver behind. This process was dangerous to the health of both humans and animals.

In the late 1800s cyanide compounds began to be used to extract silver from ore. Electricity is also used in some kinds of modern silver refining.

Silver extraction has become in-

Early miners often used animals to break up the ore, so they could extract the silver. Modern miners use drills and crushing machines to break the ore into chunks like these on a conveyor belt in a zinc and silver mine in Chihuahua, Mexico.

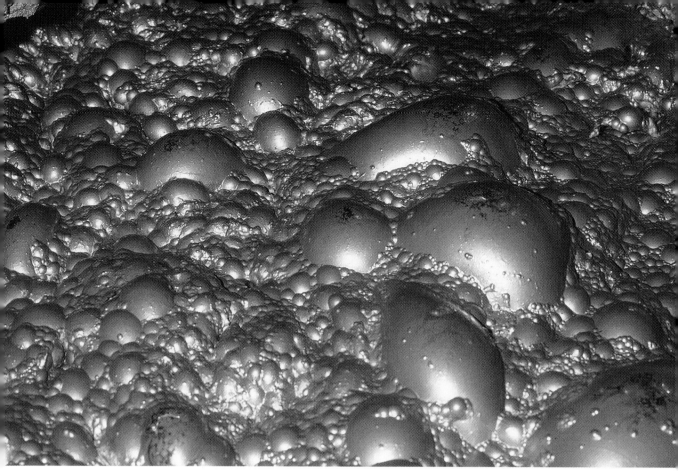

Much silver today is found in ores with other metals, and chemicals are used to separate them out. This is a chemical bath of concentrated lead and silver at a modern silver mine in Idaho.

creasingly complicated. That is because much silver today comes from recycled products, such as photographic film or old jewelry (see p. 26).

However extracted, the silver is then further refined in various ways. Copper or other materials are often added to form an alloy (see p. 9), with the amounts depending on the object to be made.

Silverworking Skills

The basic silverworking skills remained largely the same for centuries. A bar or block of silver alloy was heated (*forged*) to soften it. The silversmith then pounded it with a hammer to the right thickness.

Silver can be hammered at room temperature. However, it tends to become brittle (liable to snap or break). To make the silver tougher, it is heated again and again while being worked, a process called *annealing*.

For a bowl or other round object, the silversmith cut a circular piece from the hammered silver and hammered it into the desired shape, a process called *raising*. For large bowls or pots, the silver might be

Making this turn-of-the-20th-century brooch called for many silverworking skills. The image of Cleopatra would be made by tapping the silver from underneath (*chasing*), while some parts would be cut away to make the holes surrounding her head.

placed in a hollow wooden mold and hammered to fit the mold's shape. That is why pitchers, pots, bowls, and the like are called *hollowware*.

Other pieces, such as knives, forks, and spoons, were hammered into shape by hand from pieces of flat silver cut to the right size. That is why these are called *flatware*.

Handles, feet, spouts, and other additional pieces were often cast into molds. They would later be heated to fuse the pieces to the body of a pot or pitcher. Each form of decoration had its own special set of tools and skills.

Chasing involves pushing the silver into decorative shapes without cutting any of it away. This can be done directly on the outside of a piece. For hollowware, the silversmith used a *snarling iron*—a rod with a tiny hammer at one end—to tap the silver from the inside. This created a bulge on the outside, which was worked into the desired design.

Silver objects often have letters or symbols (*hallmarks*) on the back or bottom, identifying the maker and sometimes the owner, in this case the White Star Line (the line of the famous doomed ship *Titanic*).

Silver in the design of grapes and leaves has been formed into handles for this fine stone tray.

Engraving involves cutting a design into silver, using special sharp-edged tools. *Piercing* involves cutting out pieces of silver to make holes, as in the edge of a plate or a piece of jewelry.

These various processes can result in leftover pieces of silver. These are so valuable that they are saved for reuse. (If a silverworking shop needed a new floor, the old one would be taken up and burned for the bits of silver it contained.)

The finished silver piece was smoothed and polished to make it shine. Even so, you could often see the tiny hammer marks. Years of use by hand would make the silver even shinier, an effect that is called a *patina.*

Objects of silver were made individually by hand, so each one was unique. They were generally marked with letters or symbols (*hallmarks*), identifying the silversmith and sometimes the owner. Modern antique-lovers search for such marks to identify the source of early silver objects. Today silver objects are usually engraved or stamped with the name of a company, rather than an individual silversmith.

Modern Silverworking

Some silver objects are still made individually by specially trained silversmiths. Today, however, most silver objects are made by relatively unskilled factory workers operating machines. This change began in the

1700s, when the British developed the factory system.

Modern silversmiths create designs for silver objects. The designs are then converted into molds. The actual objects are often made by machine.

Flatware starts with strips of silver called *blanks*, pressed by heavy rollers into the desired length, width, and thickness. Other machines cut or push them into the desired shape, such as bowls for spoons. Finally a design mold is pressed onto the flatware, creating the silversmith's design.

For hollowware the silver is cast into molds, and then the design is pressed into the silver. Sometimes two halves of an object are made separately and then soldered (bonded) together, with handles and such added later. The final object is polished and smoothed with a buffing wheel.

In 1840 the British also developed a new process called *electroplating*. This allowed objects to be made of cheaper metals, such as copper, and then coated with precious metals, such as silver and gold. Objects plated with silver and gold were affordable to many more people. However, most everyday "silverware" today is made not of silver but of stainless steel.

Today some key parts of jet engines are electroplated with silver, as an extra layer of protection.

In centuries past many rich families had whole cabinets filled with silver objects like these on display in Oslo, Norway. Today, however, such items are more likely to be just plated with silver.

Silver as Money

These are two silver coins from the early Greek city of Syracuse, in what is now the Italian island of Sicily.

To make the design on each side of a coin, the early Greeks used a stamp like this one, dating from the 400s B.C. The owl shown here was a symbol generally used on coins from Athens.

Many things have been used as money, including shells, pieces of leather or porcelain (china), bars and tools of various metals—even fishhooks! However, nothing has been so widely used for money as silver coins. Gold was almost always more valued, but silver was for centuries more common in everyday coins.

King Croesus of Lydia (in what is now Turkey) is often credited with issuing the first gold and silver coins in about 560 B.C. However, coins may have been used as early as 800 B.C. in the region stretching from Egypt eastward to India and perhaps also in China.

Early coins were small, thick pieces of metal, sometimes bean-shaped but later they were more often made in the familiar circle shape. They were stamped on one and later both sides with a symbol of the ruler who issued them.

However, the problem for many centuries was that the amount of precious metal contained in coins varied. That began to change in the late 1100s, when the Venetians in Italy established a coin with a standard amount of silver, so people could know the true value of the coins. The idea spread. In about 1300 the British established a coin that had 92.5 percent silver and the rest copper for strength, later known as *sterling silver* (see p. 10).

Coins that contained different amounts of silver had different values. During the early 1800s the Mexican *peso* contained slightly more silver than equivalent American coins. As a result the peso became the favored coin in western parts of the United States. It was also the main coin used in many parts of eastern Asia, which traded heavily with Mexico at that time.

By the mid-1900s, however, the silver supply was running short. Fewer new sources were being discovered, while silver's uses were growing. Some people melted coins for the silver they contained, though it was illegal to do so. Eventually governments stopped using silver in everyday coins. In most countries today silver is only used in special collectible coins.

The "pieces of eight" that pirates sought in the 1600s and 1700s were rather rough silver coins like these, taken by modern treasure hunters from a shipwreck dating from that period.

Early photographs were made on glass plates coated with silver compounds. This is a glass plate negative of a photograph taken by Mathew Brady in the mid-1800s at the time of the Civil War.

Special Uses of Silver

As has been true for many centuries, silver continues to be widely used for jewelry and other ornamental objects. Mixed with mercury, it is also used by dentists for filling cavities. However, silver has found many new uses in the modern world.

The most important industrial use of silver is in photography. This is because some silver compounds change when exposed to light. It works this way:

Photographic film is coated with a light-sensitive silver compound. When a photographer "shoots" an image, light from the scene falls on the film. The parts that receive the most light darken, while those that receive less light stay lighter. The film is then chemically treated to stop such changes. The result is a reverse image called a *negative*, in which light shows up as dark and dark as light.

To get a photographic print (called a *positive*), light is sent through the negative onto a sheet of paper also coated with light-sensitive silver compounds. Light and dark are again reversed, and the sheet is treated with chemicals to stop further changes. The result is what we see as a photograph.

Some modern photographic processes, such as Polaroid or Xerox processes or digital cameras, do not use silver. However, the largest single industrial use of silver is still in photography.

Another major use of silver is in the electrical and electronics industries. Often mixed with other metals, such as nickel or palladium, silver is used in circuits, switches, and conductors, as in computers, other electronic equipment, storage batteries, and electrical appliances of all sorts.

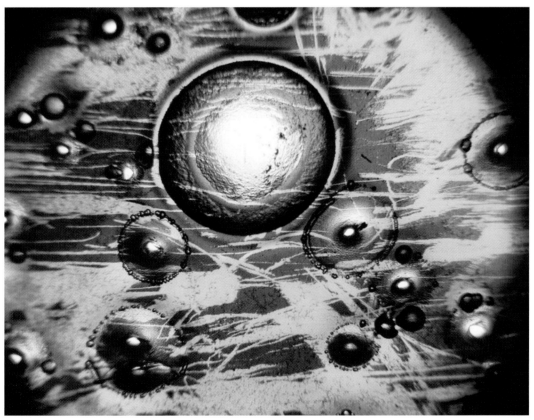

This highly magnified image shows some of the silver compounds that coat traditional kinds of film, for still or moving images. When such film is thrown away, it is often recycled to save the valuable silver for reuse.

Some modern kinds of sunglasses are coated with a silver mixture. This darkens in bright light and lightens in dimmer light to protect the eyes. This man also has silver in his mouth, in the form of a silver mixture filling his teeth.

It is even used in the embedded heated lines that keep rear automobile windshields free of frost and ice. Silver is favored for such uses because, though rare and expensive, it is such a good conductor of heat and electricity, can stand a wide range of temperatures, and does not easily corrode (see p. 7).

Silver reflects light so well that it has often been used in mirrors. In early times mirrors were simply flat pieces of metal, such as silver, polished to show a reflection. Glass mirrors with a metal coating were invented by the Venetians in the 1500s. Silver has been used as a coating for mirrors since the 1830s. Such silver coatings are also used in telescopes and a wide variety of other special equipment using lenses and mirrors.

Silver compounds have a wide-ranging role in chemical engineering. Silver is a powerful *catalyst*, a substance that helps speed a chemical change without itself being changed in the process. For example, it is used to help change chemicals from oil (petroleum) so they can be made into plastics and other materials used in modern life.

Silver compounds are also used in many chemical tests. These are called *reagents*, substances that are used to help detect and measure other substances.

Silver compounds are also used in purifying water because they fight bacteria, tiny organisms that can cause infection. For the same reason silver compounds are used in medicine, most notably as a treatment for burns.

Silver is also widely used in *brazing alloys*. These are metal compounds (typically 50 percent silver mixed with copper and zinc) used to join together pieces made of other metals, such as steel. Brazing alloys are heated to more than 430 degrees Celsius (about 800 degrees Fahrenheit). This softens the alloy so it joins the other metal pieces together. Joins using brazing alloys are often stronger than soldered joins, made at lower heats.

One of the most interesting modern uses of silver is in "seeding" clouds to make rain. Silver iodide (a compound of silver and iodine) is burned, resulting in tiny

particles. When these particles are sent up into the clouds—dropped from an airplane or shot from a rocket, for example—water in the clouds forms tiny crystals around the particles. When these crystals get large and heavy enough, they begin to fall to the earth as rain or snow.

Silver has been used in electrical and electronic circuits and for other special purposes in rockets and spaceships since the modern space program began. However, when silver is used in ships not designed to return, like this 1968 unmanned rocket, it is lost forever.

Words to Know

Ag: See ARGENTUM.

alloy A COMPOUND that includes two or more METALS.

amalgam An ALLOY containing mercury and another metal.

annealing Heating and reheating a METAL to keep it workable.

argentite The main silver-bearing ORE.

argentum The Latin and scientific name for silver, abbreviated *Ag*.

blanks: See FLATWARE.

brazing alloy A type of ALLOY used to join METAL-containing COMPOUNDS at high heat.

catalyst A substance that helps speed a chemical change without itself being changed.

chasing Pushing silver into decorative shapes.

compound A mixed material that includes two or more ELEMENTS.

conductor In chemistry, a substance through which heat or electricity easily flows.

corrode To wear away or dissolve.

crystal A naturally occurring solid that has regularly repeating flat sides.

dendrites Branching twiglike formations common in NATIVE SILVER.

ductile Soft and workable, so that it can easily be drawn into fine wire or hammered into thin sheets.

electroplating A mass-production process used to cover any metal object with a very thin sheet of silver or other metal.

electrum A naturally occurring compound of gold and silver.

elements The basic materials that make up every living and nonliving thing in the universe. Silver is an element.

engraving In SILVERSMITHING, creating a design by cutting into silver.

erosion The wearing away of the Earth's crust by wind, rain, ice, and other natural forces.

flatware (silverware) Knives, forks, and spoons shaped from a flat piece (*blank*) of METAL, such as silver, stainless steel, or metal coated with steel (see ELECTROPLATING).

forging Heating a METAL.

hallmark Letters and symbols on silver objects identifying the SILVERSMITH and sometimes the owner.

hollowware Silver objects shaped in hollow wooden molds, such as pitchers and bowls.

malleable Soft and workable, so that it is easily shaped and formed.

melting point The temperature at which a substance melts. Silver melts at 962 degrees Celsius (about 1764 degrees Fahrenheit).

metal A group of ELEMENTS that includes silver. Most metals are good CONDUCTORS, and they often easily form COMPOUNDS with other elements. Usually solid at room temperature, they can often be hammered into desired shapes or melted and poured into desired shapes.

native silver Pure or nearly pure silver found in nature.

negative: See PHOTOGRAPHY.

noble metals Silver, gold, platinum, and other metals that do not readily form COMPOUNDS with other substances.

ore A natural rock formation that contains a desired substance.

patina The shine given to silver that has had long and heavy use.

patio process A Native-American method of extracting silver, using mules to crush the ORE, then extracting silver by adding mercury and other substances.

photography The process of producing an image on light-sensitive surfaces, often using film coated with light-sensitive silver COMPOUNDS to create a reverse image called a *negative*, which is then used to make a *positive*, the image we see as a photograph.

piercing In SILVERSMITHING, creating a design by cutting out bits of silver.

positive: See PHOTOGRAPHY.

precious metals METALS so valuable that they are used for jewelry and coinage.

raising In SILVERSMITHING, hammering an object into the desired shape, often using a tiny hammer called a *snarling iron*.

reagent A substance that is used to help detect and measure other substances.

silversmith An artist and craftsperson who creates works made of silver.

silverware: See FLATWARE.

smelting The process of melting an ORE to separate out one or more desired METALS.

snarling iron: See RAISING.

sterling silver A high-quality silver mixture that contains at least 925 parts (92.5 percent) silver out of 1,000.

tarnishing Discoloration and dulling.

On the Internet

The Internet has many interesting sites about silver. The site addresses often change, so the best way to find current addresses is to go to a search site, such as www.yahoo.com. Type in a word or phrase, such as "silver."

As this book was being written, websites about silver included:

http://www.silverinstitute.org/
Silver Institute website, offering information on history and current uses and production, plus links to related sites and online version of *Silver News*.

http://minerals.er.usgs.gov/minerals/pubs/commodity/silver/index.html
U.S. Geological Survey Minerals Information section on Silver.

http://www.silvermag.com/SILVER.HTM
Silver Magazine website, with online versions of current and back issues.

http://www.nationalgeographic.com/silverbank/index.html
Silver Bank, a section of the National Geographic Society website, offering a virtual tour of the Spanish silver ship *Concepción*, taken by pirates in 1641.

http://www.museumca.org/goldrush/silver.html
Silver and Gold, section of a site from California's Oakland Museum.

In Print

Your local library system will have various books on silver. The following is just a sampling of them.

Chase, Sara Hannum. *The First Book of Silver*. New York: Franklin Watts, 1969.

Franck, Irene M., and David M. Brownstone. *Manufacturers and Miners*. New York: Facts On File, 1989. Part of the Work Throughout History series.

Hood, Graham. *American Silver: A History of Style, 1650–1900*. New York: E. P. Dutton, 1989.

Knauth, Percy. *The Metalsmiths*. Alexandria, VA: Time-Life Books, 1974.

Lister, Raymond. *The Craftsman in Metal*. South Brunswick, NJ/New York: A. S. Barnes, 1966.

St. John, Jeffrey. *Noble Metals*. Alexandria, VA: Time-Life Books, 1984.

Stwertka, Albert. *Oxford Guide to the Elements*. New York: Oxford, 1998.

Van Nostrand's Scientific Encyclopedia, 8th ed., 2 vols. Douglas M. Considine and Glenn D. Considine, eds. New York: Van Nostrand Reinhold, 1995.

Watkins, Tom H. *Gold and Silver in the West: The Illustrated History of an American Dream*. Palo Alto, CA: American West, 1971.

Index